Rooted

Building a Classroom from the Ground Up

Published by Tupou Leadership Group

ISBN: 979-8-9944217-0-3

Cover illustration by Uinimila Grewe

Content edited by Hancock Publishers

Printed in the United States of America

First Edition

For more information follow

@TupouLeadership on social media

www.tupouleadershipgroup.com

Contents

Acknowledgments

I want to thank my husband, Otini, for allowing me the time and emotional support through my master's program, working, and writing this book. My husband is such an amazing support, and I don't know what I would do without him. Thank you, my love, for all that you do for me and for our babies.

I want to thank Sione and Elizabeth for fully supporting me as their mamma with so much love and motivation, from the hugs and kisses to the handmade posters on the doors of my room reminding me "one chapter a day." Through the writing and through the editing, it feels like we did it together. I love and appreciate y'all so much for that.

I want to thank my mommy Janet, Shani, and my father-in-law Paula for showing me that being a business owner is possible.

My **entire** family is amazing and the ultimate support system. Parents and family—if you're reading this, I love you. Thank you for all the love and support.

Thank you to the many leaders who have influenced me. My principal Adrian—thank you for being such an amazing and inspirational leader. I'm also so grateful for all my assistant principals along the way. Mr. Perrett, thank you especially for all your positivity, honesty and always pushing me to go above and beyond. Thank you to all the teachers I have been blessed to work with. Speakers like Brian Mendler and Ms. Squirrel have truly made an impact on me and the decisions I make in my classroom.

To my best friend Belen, for always pouring into me on a weekly basis, fueling me with positivity. She has no idea how much good our conversations have led to.

My grandparents are no longer living, but I hope that I am making them proud.

Thank you to my two co-teachers over the years, Mr. Adams and Mr. Pullen, for allowing me to be my best self with full acceptance—**and for listening to me ramble about everything that's written in this book**...Before it was even written. Thank y'all for fully supporting my ideas from day 1. Y'all are great!

Thank you to my district Math specialist, Michelle Merritt, for allowing me opportunities to lead professional development sessions outside of just my school. The knowledge and experience I have gained from them have been incredible and very much appreciated.

Thank you to Uinimila Grewe for taking my vision of *Rooted* and bringing it to life with the cover of the book as well as the logo for Tupou Leadership Group, LLC. When she sent me the final drawing, I felt the joy in my heart, especially the roots. And that's the whole entire point—starting from the ground up with everything: family, business, teaching, and life in general. The roots are key, and I truly appreciate her bringing my vision to life with this image.

Thank you to every person who has ever told me I've inspired you or made you smile. Mrs. Oliva, thank you for your constant encouragement to put my work out there.

To my team, thank you all for all of your encouraging words and being the reasons I want to do better. Thank you to the teachers who provided me input on the pencil situation that starts chapter 1.

Thank you. Thank you. Thank you. *Thank you all* from the bottom of my heart.

Preface

Becoming More than the Role

I was sitting in a professional development session, one I signed up for on my own, outside of what was required, full of excitement. I was in the middle of my second year of teaching, still figuring out how to keep my head above water, still hungry for something I couldn't quite name.

There was a speaker at the front of the room. She had a doctorate degree. She was talking about leadership, about education, about something that made my heart do jumping jacks inside my chest. Although I can't recall a single specific word she said, I can tell you exactly what I felt as the speaker spoke.

I felt seen, inspired, and motivated. It felt like someone had reached across the room and whispered, "You could do this too."

I left that session buzzing with something I'd never experienced before—not just inspiration, but direction. I immediately called my sister and told her, "I want to get my doctorate!" My sister quickly reminded me that I needed my master's first (laughing now). I had spent 10 years working towards my bachelor's, and before this moment, I was done with college—or so I thought. I was that inspired and motivated to become more than the role I was in after that leadership workshop. The next day, I enrolled in my master's program at Lamar University. I didn't have a five-year plan. I didn't even know exactly what I was chasing. I just knew I wanted to become the kind of educator who could stand in front of a room and make someone else feel what I'd just felt. I'm getting watery-eyed just writing this. This is why I'm writing this book...

Looking back now, I realize what shifted in me that day. I discovered that teaching wasn't just about what happens in my classroom. It was about building something bigger than lesson plans and procedures. It's about building leaders.

Here's what I've learned since that day:

Most of us didn't go into teaching because we love paperwork, behavior management, or explaining the same concept seventeen different ways. We went into teaching because we believed we could make a difference.

Somewhere between the first-year survival mode and the daily grind of demands, deadlines, and decision fatigue, our belief in making a difference gets buried under stress, overwhelm, and exhaustion.

We start wondering: Is this sustainable? Am I doing enough? Why does everything feel so hard? I know, because I've been there.

I've been the teacher standing in front of a class, reading 25 Pinterest procedures off a sheet of paper, convinced I had it all figured out, only to watch everything fall apart a few days later.

I've been the teacher yelling so much that I would go home with a sore throat every single day.

I've been the teacher walking in circles around my desk with seventeen browser tabs open (in my head and on my computer), completely paralyzed by overwhelm, wondering if I was truly cut out for this.

And I've also been the teacher who figured out that small, intentional systems could transform not just my classroom but my entire experience of teaching. The teacher who learned that relationships aren't "extra"; they are the foundation of everything. The teacher who discovered that protecting my own energy by creating boundaries wasn't selfish, it was survival. The teacher who realized that when I took care of myself, I showed up better for my students.

This book exists because of that professional development session where I felt something shift inside me. But it also exists because of every moment since then—every procedure I've refined, every relationship I've built, every boundary I've learned to set, and every time I've chosen to walk the hallway instead of spiraling at my desk.

It exists because I've sat across from burned-out teachers in professional development sessions I've led and watched them realize, "I don't have to keep doing it the hard way."

It exists because I've seen the relief on teachers' faces when I tell them: You're not failing. You just need different tools.

This book is the conversation I wish I could have had with myself six years ago when I was drowning. It's the mentor session I needed when I thought procedures were something you read off a piece of paper. It's the resource I wish every new teacher had access to. It's the permission slip I wish someone had handed me to stop trying to be superhuman.

If you're reading this, I'm guessing you're somewhere on that journey too. Maybe you're in survival mode, wondering if you'll make it to the next break. Maybe you've been teaching for years, but something feels off and you can't figure out what. Maybe you're inspired and hungry for more, just like I was in that session. Or maybe you're about to enter your first year of teaching. Wherever you are, this book is for you.

Not because I have all the answers, but because I've walked this road, made the mistakes, learned the lessons, and figured out what actually works—not in theory, but in real classrooms with real students.

This book is full of practical strategies, neuroscience research, and honest stories from my own classroom. But more than that, it's a reminder that you don't have to choose between being an excellent teacher and being a whole human.

You can be both.

- You can build a classroom where students thrive *and* protect your own peace.
- You can be the teacher who inspires students *and* goes home with energy left for your own family.
- You can love teaching *and* set boundaries.
- You can be a leader *and* still be learning.

So here's what I want you to know before you turn the page:

You don't need to be superhuman.

You don't need to have it all figured out.

You don't need to sacrifice yourself to be a good teacher.

What you need are practical tools, grounded strategies, and permission to do things differently.

That's what this book is about.

Let's get rooted together—building something sustainable, one small, intentional shift at a time.

Because when we all become teacher leaders, educators who empower ourselves and each other, our schools become better places. Our students become more successful. Our communities become stronger.

And it starts with you, taking care of yourself so you can show up fully for the work that matters.

Welcome. I'm so glad you're here. Let's begin.

Introduction

We don't just teach content. We teach the minds and hearts of our students. And that is where my passion lies.

This book is organized around one core principle: **sustainable teaching starts with small, intentional systems.**

What you'll find in this book:

- Not 25 procedures you found on Pinterest.
- Not working yourself into the ground
- Not choosing between being an excellent teacher and being a whole human.
- You can have both and this book will show you how.

Here's the journey we're going on together.

Build the Foundation

We start with the thing that broke me: a pencil. You'll learn why small procedures save your mental energy—and your students' mental energy—and how to build systems that create independence instead of dependence. Then we dive into relationships, because procedures without relationships are just rules. And rules without trust don't work.

Protect What Goes In

You can't pour from an empty cup, but you also can't pour from a cup filled with poison. In this chapter, we talk about consumption—what you're feeding yourself mentally, emotionally, and physically—because what you consume shapes how you show up.

Protect What Goes Out

Boundaries aren't selfish. They're survival. This chapter is about learning to say no, stop taking work home, and protect your nervous system so you can show up whole for your students—and your own family..

Put it All Together

Now we get practical. Chapter 5 walks you through the first weeks of school, week by week, so you know exactly what to do and when. Chapter 6 is about what happens when things fall apart, because they will. You'll learn how to troubleshoot procedures, how to discipline with dignity, and how to choose Option 2 instead of exploding in front of your students.

Sustain Yourself

This is the chapter I wish I'd had six years ago. You'll learn micro-moments of self-care that fit into your actual workday. You'll explore two-minute strategies that reset your nervous system between classes. This chapter comes from a professional development session I co-led where teachers told me: "This session was just what I needed."

The Foundation You've Built

We close with perspective. On hard days, you need to remember that you don't have to be superhuman. You don't have to have it all figured out. You just need to show up, grounded and whole, for the work that matters.

What Makes This Book Different

I'm not a researcher sitting in an ivory tower.

I am not all-knowing of everything there is to know. I'm not a professional writer. I am a teacher. A team leader. A master's-level educator. A mom. A wife. A woman who almost lost herself to this profession—and who found a way back. And someone who is very passionate about the systems you will receive in this book.

This book is grounded in three things:

1. **Real classroom experience.** Every strategy, every procedure, every story comes from my actual classroom with real students. I've made the mistakes. I've learned the lessons. I've figured out what works—not in theory, but in practice.

2. **Brain science that makes sense.** Throughout this book, you'll see grey boxes with neuroscience research explaining *why* these strategies work… Because when you understand the brain science behind classroom management, relationships, and self-care, you stop second-guessing yourself and trust the process.

3. **Honest, practical tools.** This book is full of journaling prompts, step-by-step procedures, and strategies you can implement tomorrow. Not someday —tomorrow.

The preface told you why this book exists, now here's how to use it…

You can read this book cover to cover, and I hope you do. Each chapter builds on the last. The journaling prompts shouldn't be optional. This is where the real work happens. The grey boxes with the neuroscience? Read them. They'll help you trust the process when it feels hard.

But you can also:

- Skip to the chapter that speaks to your current struggle.
- Use the journaling prompts as morning pages before students arrive or during your conference period.
- Dog-ear the pages that resonate and come back to them when you need them.

- Share sections with your team, your mentor, or your teacher friends.

This book is a *conversation*, not a lecture.

If you're reading this mid-year, exhausted and wondering if you can make it one more semester, start with Chapter 7. Learn how to take care of yourself at work, not just after you've survived the day.

If you're reading this in the summer, preparing for a fresh school year, start with Chapters 1 and 2. Build your foundation before the chaos starts.

If you're reading this and you're drowning, skip to Chapter 4. Set one boundary. Protect one hour. You'll be amazed at what shifts.

A Final Word Before We Begin

I had to give a speech for a submission and chance to win District Teacher of the Year. In that speech, I closed with this:

"You are the light of the world. A town built on a hill cannot be hidden. Neither do people light a lamp and put it under a bowl. Instead, they put it on its stand, and it gives light to everyone in the house. In the same way, let your light shine before others, that they may see your good deeds and glorify your Father in heaven" —Matthew 5:14-16

You are the light of the world, but you can't shine if you're burning out.

You can't give light to everyone in the house if you're running on empty.

This book exists to help you protect that light, build systems that sustain it, and create a classroom where students thrive—and so do you.

Your classroom is waiting. Your students are waiting. And so is the version of you who can do this work and still have energy left for your own life.

Turn the page. Let's build something sustainable. Let's get rooted.

Chapter 1

The Pencil That Broke Me!

Picture this: You've taken the time and planned an amazing lesson for the day. Students walk into your classroom, and before they even begin the warm-up, you're interrupted with:

> "Miss, I don't have a pencil."
> "Can I borrow a pencil?"
> "Do you have an extra pencil?"

Five minutes—gone. Your carefully planned warm-up... derailed! Sound familiar? This was me for about two years into my teaching career until I couldn't mentally take it anymore. I was so beyond frustrated. Over pencils!

I asked a few teachers on my campus what it sounds like in their classrooms when students ask for pencils at the beginning of class. A few responses were:

> "I need a pencil."
> "Do you have a pencil I can use all day?"
> "Are there any extra pencils?"

One teacher responded by saying, "Sometimes the students ask quietly for a pencil, yet others wait until the last second to ask for one." Meaning, they sat there doing nothing and waited until they decided they were ready to ask for a pencil.

I was extremely frustrated with this pencil situation because I wanted the beginning of my class to run smoothly—no issues, every day. I wanted the students to come into the classroom, sit down, take out their materials, and begin their warm-up without needing me. I wanted my 6th graders to be independent for the first 5 minutes so I could mentally adjust to the start of the class.

But how could they? This is the age where their prefrontal cortex isn't fully developed. They're not fully capable of staying organized or keeping track of their things. So how could I get upset with them over pencils when it's not entirely their fault?

And then I realized something. They can do it. If they can learn how to navigate a video game or figure out where to go when they walk into the school building, they can learn how to handle needing a pencil without derailing my peace.

JOURNALING PROMPT:

Take a minute to jot down what frustrates you on a daily or weekly basis within your classroom. (Think about what and when your students are asking you for things):

_____

_____

_____

_____

_____

The issue for me? The pencil. Problem identified. Solution: Create a procedure for students who need a pencil.

As I tell my students on the first day of school, "A procedure is just an official way of doing something—operating instructions." I explain, "These procedures are in place to help you manage your own learning, and so no one is confused at any time about what to do in certain situations." (Feel free to use the same wording in your classroom!)

I hope you took the two minutes to write about something that frustrates you in your classroom. This will help you identify a problem you didn't realize needed a solution. What's important to you? What frustrates you if it's not done a certain way? Take note somewhere on this page so you can reference it later! If you're a first-year teacher, you may not know yet—but as soon as you do, this is where you start. If you've been in the classroom at least one school year, I'm sure you have an idea of what frustrates you or how you'd prefer things done.

As for me in my classroom, I like to explain to students what a procedure is. I don't want the stigma of procedures to be anything negative, so I explain that it's simply a set of steps to be taken for any given situation. The purpose of a procedure is so that no one is confused at any time about what to do. For example, in my classroom, it really bothers me when students come into class and tell me they don't have a pencil. Why does that bother me? Not having a pencil is not the issue. I am aware of the many school supplies students do not have, and I understand the financial struggles some families face. I'm also aware that students struggle to keep track of things. So, not having a pencil is not the issue. The issue is their need to tell me—when the first five minutes of class should be spent working on their warm-up, and they should not need me for any reason, unless it's an emergency, of course. That is the expectation. That is my expectation. Find your expectations…

So, how did I get my students to do what they needed to do while leaving me out of it? I established a procedure for pencils. I have this printed on a sheet of paper and posted by the pencil jar.

Procedure for needing a pencil

1. Take a pencil from the jar.
2. Sign your name on the sheet provided (usually a notepad we continue to use all year).
3. At the end of the class period, cross out your name.
4. Return the pencil to the jar.

Sounds so simple, right? But this was a drastic change in the dynamic of my classroom. And here's why it worked—not just logistically, but neurologically.

What is happening?

Students are independent and, without realizing it, displaying self-responsibility by recognizing they need something and following the procedure independently to take care of their need. They are building confidence. Several students are afraid to speak up, especially to adults. In this case, they don't have to. The fear of asking for a pencil is gone when they can successfully get one by themselves.

Why is this important?

This is important because it's important to me. What's important to you? I want the first five minutes of class to be quiet, controlled, and purposeful.

JOURNALING PROMPT

Take a moment: What do you need your students to be able to do on their own in the first five minutes of class? What would allow you to enter your lesson feeling clear and calm instead of frazzled and reactive? Write it down—no judgment, just honesty.

_____

_____

_____

_____

_____

Now let's talk about the brain science behind why you need this...

The brain science behind it:

What's happening in your brain (the teacher)? Research shows that teachers make over 1,000 decisions per day. Every interruption—"I need a pencil"—is a micro-decision that drains your mental energy. When students are independent during the first few minutes, you preserve your cognitive resources for the actual teaching ahead.

The student? Students also have limited cognitive capacity. When they walk into chaos and don't know what to do, their brains are spending energy on: What do I need? What are we doing? Am I in trouble? Having a procedure for something as simple as a pencil eliminates five or more micro-decisions. Students know exactly what to do—no guessing, no anxiety. That saves their mental energy, which can now be directed toward learning during the warm-up. Educational research confirms that students with executive function challenges (ADHD, trauma, etc.) especially need this structure.

Nervous system regulation: For you — Neuroscience shows that chaos and unpredictability activate your stress response (sympathetic nervous system). In contrast, order and predictability help keep your nervous system calm and regulated.

For the student: Many students arrive at your class already dysregulated—hungry, anxious, overstimulated, and/or traumatized. (This brings me back to Maslow's good ol' hierarchy of needs!) Research on trauma and child development confirms that predictable environments help regulate the nervous system.

Mental clarity: For you — Your prefrontal cortex (the "CEO of your brain") handles planning, decision-making, and emotional regulation. Brain research shows it works best when not overwhelmed.

For the student: Developmental neuroscience confirms that a student's prefrontal cortex (especially in middle schoolers) is still developing and has less executive function capacity than an adult's. When procedures remove decisions, their limited executive function can focus on "What's 7 x 8?" instead of "What am I supposed to be doing right now?" Studies show that students with ADHD, autism, or learning disabilities benefit enormously from reduced cognitive load.

Bottom line: Research across psychology and neuroscience confirms that predictability removes stress—for both you and the student.

WOW! No wonder I feel so awesome going into my lessons now. It's because of the mental energy saved for my lessons. It makes me think about the stress I had during my second year. That year was the worst! I mean, I was yelling every day at my students, so much so that I would go home with a sore throat daily! I can laugh about it now (I'm giggling actually). Yet, I am grateful for the struggle I went through and the knowledge I gained from it, which I can now share with you. But I was a mess! My class was a mess! My students thought it was funny, and I

8

was angry. Let's not talk about how stress affects your body and longevity—I could probably write a whole book on that alone.

How much time is wasted if students come into class trying to find a pencil from their classmates or just sitting there because either they don't want to ask for a pencil or they're scared? Having a procedure in place for pencils takes away any barriers and excuses. It allows me as the teacher to use this time to acclimate to the new set of students, take attendance, or have whatever self-care moment I need.

Additional Procedures

The pencil procedure is one of many in my classroom that contributes to the success and peace of mind I have. There is also a procedure for when students do not have their homework.

I collect homework daily while the students are completing their warm-up/do-now assignment. The expectation is that their homework is on their desk, visible, so I do not need to bother them or take their attention away from their task. The procedure is: If students know they do not have or did not complete their homework, they grab a pink slip on the way in and complete it with a short explanation of why they don't have their homework.

Again, they are learning to take responsibility. Sometimes, just knowing they will have to turn in a pink slip actually motivates them to ensure their homework is completed the night before. We also have a procedure for entering the classroom, what to do if a student needs to get up for any reason, and a procedure for handling mistakes. There is a procedure for it all.

The Question That Changed Everything

My first year of teaching, once the students were all physically in the classroom and had signed their expectation contracts (you will learn more about these later), the teaching began—or so I thought. I began having behavior issues, with one student in particular. I remember feeling so frustrated and angry because this student would not follow any of my directions. He would talk back, lean back in his chair instead of keeping all four legs on the floor—just disobedient, or so I thought. I went to my team leader and explained what was going on, like some nerve this student had to be disrespectful and act up in *my* classroom.

My team leader asked me a question that lingered in my head for years. She asked, "Did you teach him—the class—the procedures?"

You remember that specific sheet of paper I told you about and that contract I had my students sign? Well, I confidently answered, "Yeah, I told them the expectations!" In my mind, I wanted to add that they had also signed the contracts saying they understood all the expectations and procedures.

10

Then, she asked me again, with more emphasis: "Did you TEACH them the procedures and expectations?"

As a brand-new teacher, standing there scratching my head, confused, I thought, *What is she talking about, teach? What does that even mean?* I'm laughing now, but at the time, I had no idea what she meant, and that was the end of that conversation. I don't believe it ever came up again, as far as I can remember.

The year went on—typical first year of teaching—yet the behavior continued to be an issue every single day.

The Aha Moment

Fast forward to my second year of teaching: I was losing control in my classroom. New school, new year, different students, but the same issues. At the time, I didn't have any procedures set in stone, so the students didn't know what to do for certain things. This is when my pencil procedure was developed. That was the one thing I could have the students do on their own, without involving me. It relieved the mental load from me, and I didn't realize it would also relieve the mental load for them.

I was in a portable classroom that year, and when it was time for the students to be dismissed, they would literally run out and down the ramp to the door of the school. No big deal, right?

Well, little did I know (until I knew) that when they got to the building, they would bang on the doors—which was ridiculous! But, of course, they would! Why not? I never told them otherwise. I never told them what to do when they left my classroom. I never showed them.

The Brain Science Behind Teaching Expectations

The developing prefrontal cortex: Developmental neuroscience confirms that the prefrontal cortex—responsible for impulse control, planning, and predicting consequences—isn't fully developed until the mid-20s. Middle schoolers literally cannot always predict, "If I do this, that will happen." Their brains need explicit teaching.

Executive function and transfer: Research shows that even if students have learned expectations in one context (e.g., "Don't run in the hallway at their old school"), they may not automatically transfer that knowledge to a new setting. Their brains need to be taught the expectation *in context*.

How the brain learns patterns (schemas): Cognitive psychology shows that the brain learns through schemas—mental frameworks for how things work. Without a schema for "how dismissal works in this classroom," students' brains default to guessing. Explicit teaching builds the schema.

The brain fills in gaps: Neuroscience confirms that the brain hates uncertainty and fills in gaps with whatever makes sense. If you don't teach the expectation, students' brains assume: "No one stopped me, so this must be fine."

The assumption gap: Educational psychology highlights the disconnect between what adults assume students know and what students actually know. Research shows that closing this gap with clear expectations reduces behavior issues—not because students are "better behaved," but because their brains now have the information they need.

Bottom line: Kids aren't being defiant—they literally don't know what you expect unless you teach them.

And here, in this moment, was when I understood what my team leader from the year before meant!

I had to *teach* them my procedures and expectations.

Teaching Procedures Explicitly

So, the following first day of school, I taught my dismissal procedure explicitly. My second-year procedure looked like this:

Dismissal Procedure:

1. When the bell rings, stay seated until I dismiss you.
2. Line up at the corner of the ramp (if someone goes early, they return to the line and wait).
3. Walk (don't run) down the ramp.
4. Wait quietly at the building door until I open the door.

I explain and model it, then we practice it (multiple times). And guess what? No more door-banging, and no more running down the ramp. The next four years, my dismissal procedure changed since my classroom was inside the building. So, the classroom procedure I am going to share with you now is my procedure for entering the classroom. No gatekeeping here.

Entering the Classroom Procedure:

1. Enter into the classroom and go directly to your seat.
2. Unpack your materials for the day (folder, notebook, and writing tools).

3. Go directly to the backpack hooks and hang your backpack (I do not like students being distracted by what's in their backpacks during lesson time)
4. Go to your seat and begin the warm-up quietly

I explain this procedure explicitly on the first day of school. I teach it by actually practicing it. This looks like us going back into the hallway with our belongings, where we practice entering and going straight to the students' desks. There, they practice unpacking their materials and hanging up their backpacks. They get to experience sitting down and starting their first warm-up.

I check for understanding. "Someone raise your hand and let me know, what is the first thing we are supposed to do when we enter the classroom?" I do this for each step until I'm confident they've got it.

The following day, I let them know I'm watching to make sure everyone remembers. It's amazing! This, along with my pencil procedure, is gold! I get my mental clarity in the first five minutes of class, and they get theirs.

And to be honest, it's kind of cool when someone walks by, and all my students are seated and doing what they are supposed to do by the tardy bell, despite the commotion outside our classroom.

That's the power of teaching expectations explicitly.

Procedures aren't about control—they're about creating the mental space you need to actually teach.

JOURNALING PROMPT:

Identifying Your Assumptions

What expectation do you have that you've never explicitly taught because you assumed students "should just know"?

(Examples: how to enter the room, what to do when they finish early, how to ask for help, how to pack up.)

Write it down, then commit to teaching it explicitly this week.

_____

_____

_____

_____

Chapter 2:

Building Relationships That Actually Matter

Picture this: I stood in front of my first class like a queen on a stage addressing her subjects, hand waving regally, as I read off 25 classroom procedures I'd found on Pinterest and Instagram. My students had signed contracts! I was *so* proud.

And then…everything fell apart. Let me explain.

My first year of teaching—the year after everyone left for COVID. As a new teacher, of course, we had the professional development meetings, staff meetings, new teacher orientation, and all the rest. I remember being super excited. I was finally a teacher, ready to change lives and conquer the world.

I remember one specific sheet of paper that was given to me to fill out and submit to my administrator before the first day of school. Here I was, brand new, and the title of this sheet of paper was "Classroom Procedures."

"Okay, I got this," I thought. "No problem! Pinterest, here I come!"

I looked on Pinterest, Instagram, and any other social media to find cool ideas and procedures for my classroom (laughing now). To be honest, in hindsight, I can't tell you one thing that I wrote on that paper. But I was ready! The paper was filled out with about 25 procedures for different things, with a little contract I made to go along with it (I think I saw this on Instagram).

When the students returned to school mid-year (hybrid at this point, some online and some in class), I stood on that stage (it felt like a stage), in front of the class, and read that paper with the list of procedures so proudly! Then I told the class, "Congratulations! Today is a big day — you will be signing your first contract!"

I was so proud of the procedures I wrote down, and like a queen, I stood in front of the room reading them off to the students. BAM — contracts signed! And done. On to my first day of teaching with students actually in front of me in a classroom.

The students signed their classroom procedure contracts (the contracts said something like, "You have been reading the classroom procedures, and you have said you agree to this; your signature proves that you agree"). We began the lesson. It took me no more than about 5 minutes total to read and for them to sign, and maybe an additional minute for me to pick up the contracts. Then learning began—or so I thought!

What I Wish I Could Tell My Younger Self

If I could go back to that year, or better yet, if I could sit with myself back then over a cup of coffee and break down what I should have done with a list and detailed instructions on how to have a better first day—or better, any day—I would tell my old self exactly what I'm going to tell you now. Yes, you! (Smile).

I would tell myself: Before you worry about procedures, before you stress about lesson plans, you need to build the foundation. And that foundation is relationship.

Expectations vs. Reality

In my first year of teaching, I didn't go into the classroom teaching rules and procedures or building relationships. I didn't realize the importance of these until my second year of teaching. I thought classroom management meant having the right list of rules and "things to do." I thought if students just signed a contract agreeing to my expectations, they'd follow them.

I was wrong.

What I didn't understand was that students can't—and won't—follow expectations from a teacher they don't trust. They won't learn from a teacher they don't like. And they definitely won't respect procedures when they haven't been seen, heard, or valued as human beings first.

How to Begin (and Not Necessarily on Day One)

I was sitting in a new teacher meeting for my second year of teaching, in a different district and school than my first year, when the speaker said something that has stayed with me ever since. I'm passing this on to you, although this may not be new news:

Students don't learn from teachers they don't like.

Now, my first year of teaching, this would have made no sense to me. But let me explain.

We went through a mini session answering four questions:

- How do you think you should treat the teacher?
- How should the teacher treat you?
- How should you treat each other?
- How should we all treat the classroom?

I have done this since day one of my second year of teaching, and I would have told myself six years ago to do this as well.

The students were the ones answering these questions, not me!

My first year doing this, one student (she ended up always being in school suspension — ISS) said, and I quote: "Wow, no one has ever asked me how I wanted to be treated before!"

My life was forever changed.

Who knew that asking the students how they wanted to be treated would be such a big deal? But it was incredibly impactful, and it shaped our classroom.

The Brain Science Behind Relationships & Learning

Why students can't learn from teachers they don't like: Neuroscience research shows that the brain constantly scans for safety versus threat. When students feel disrespected or unseen, the amygdala (the brain's threat detection center) activates, and the brain shifts into survival mode. In survival mode, the prefrontal cortex—responsible for learning and memory—goes offline. Students literally cannot learn effectively when they feel unsafe.

The neuroscience of belonging: Studies confirm that belonging is a fundamental human need. When students feel valued, their brains release oxytocin and dopamine, creating optimal conditions for learning. When they feel excluded, stress hormones like cortisol impair memory and cognition.

Autonomy and motivation: Research in Self-Determination Theory shows that autonomy (having a voice and choice) activates the brain's reward centers and increases intrinsic motivation. When students co-create classroom agreements, they're more invested because their brains recognize: "I helped make this."

Psychological safety: Educational psychology research confirms that students need psychological safety to take intellectual risks—asking questions, making mistakes, and engaging deeply. Without it, the brain stays in self-protection mode, and higher-order thinking becomes nearly impossible.

The power of being seen: Developmental psychology shows that being acknowledged and valued is critical for healthy identity development. For many students, being asked "How do you want to be treated?" is the first time an adult has communicated: You matter. Your voice matters.

Bottom line: Research across psychology and neuroscience confirms that relationships aren't just "nice to have"—they're neurologically essential for learning.

Building the Roots: Treatment Agreements

The first thing I would have told myself six years ago, and I'm telling you now, is that it is never too late to establish how everyone should be treated in your classroom. This is the beginning of building culture and the foundation for positive engagement and learning to take place.

I have done this on the first day of school every year since. It's my non-negotiable. I even give students the opportunity to add to our "treatment agreement" after Thanksgiving break because sometimes it takes a few months for students to feel safe enough to speak up. By this time, they've also gotten to know each other a bit more.

Every year there are similarities, and there are differences. Here's what our most recent treatment agreement looked like:

Treatment Agreement

Students to Students
- Don't be mean
- Be kind
- Be grateful for each other
- Be respectful to each other
- Treat like siblings or friends
- Like friends
- Treat others like you want to be treated
- Be caring
- Treat each other equally
- Don't swear, hurt or hit anyone
- Care, love and respect each other

Students to Teacher
- Be nice
- Be respectful
- the way we want to be treated
- kind

Teacher to Students
- Be kind
- Nice
- Respectful to everyone
- Be fun
- Like their own child
- Respect the students and be kind all the time
- No yelling
- No hands on students

Students & Teacher to Classroom
- Be kind by picking up our own mess
- Fun/happy attitude, talk in private with a teacher if needed
- With respect by not breaking anything
- By not messing anything up
- By respecting each others space
- Keep things organized
- Respect rules/boundaries
- Don't steal

2025-2026 Classroom Treatment Agreement

23

These agreements are ours! The roots of our classroom.

When you build the foundation of mutual respect and psychological safety, everything else—procedures, management, even academic rigor—becomes possible. Because now, students' brains are open to learning.

JOURNALING PROMPT:

If your students could be brutally honest with you, what do you think they would say they need from you that they're not getting?

_____

_____

_____

_____

_____

_____

Seeing the Whole Student: Understanding Maslow's Hierarchy in Your Classroom

Here's something I learned that transformed how I see my students: relationships aren't just about being nice or building rapport. They're about understanding what your students actually need to be able to learn.

You've probably heard of Maslow's hierarchy of needs, but let me tell you how it showed up in my classroom in a way that changed everything.

Maya's Story

I had a student—let's call her Maya—who was struggling. Not just academically, but emotionally. She would come to class withdrawn, sometimes tearful, other times angry. Her work was inconsistent. Some days she'd engage fully; other days she'd put her head down and refuse to participate.

I could have labeled her as "difficult" or "unmotivated." But instead, I started paying attention.

One day, she stayed after class and opened up to me. She was struggling with feeling unloved by her mother. She had lost some close friends. She was dealing with grief and rejection that had nothing to do with my math class—but everything to do with whether she could actually learn in it.

That's when Maslow's hierarchy became real for me.

The Hierarchy Explained:

1. **Physiological needs (bottom level):** Food, water, shelter, sleep — the basics for survival.
2. **Safety needs:** Physical safety, security, stability
3. **Love and Belonging:** Connection, friendships, feeling valued.
4. **Esteem needs:** Feelings of accomplishment, confidence, respect.
5. **Self-actualization (top level):** Achieving your full potential.

The Realization

Here's what I realized: Maya was stuck at level 3—Love and Belonging. No amount of excellent teaching, engaging lessons, or high expectations was going to help her reach level 5 (self-actualization in math) when she couldn't even get her love and belonging needs met.

How can we expect students to learn algebra when they don't feel safe or loved? How can they focus on their warm-up when they're hungry? How can they achieve their potential when they don't feel like they belong?

We can't.

My job wasn't just to teach Maya how to solve equations. My job was to help create the conditions where she could actually access learning. And that started with seeing where she was stuck and finding ways—small, manageable ways—to help meet those needs in my classroom. So, after understanding this, then what? What does it look like when you make adjustments according to Maslow?

What This Looks Like in Practice:

For physiological needs: Keep snacks available. Don't make a big deal about it. Just have them. Notice if a student seems tired or unfocused and offer grace instead of consequences.

For safety needs: Be predictable. Be consistent. Don't embarrass students publicly. Create a classroom where mistakes are expected and respected, not shamed.

For love and belonging: This is where your treatment agreement comes in. This is where greeting students at the door matters. This is where knowing their names, their interests, and their stories makes all the difference. Make them feel like they belong in your room.

For esteem needs: Celebrate effort, not just achievement. Give students opportunities to succeed. Notice when they're trying, even if they're not there yet.

For self-actualization: Once the foundation is there, this is where learning happens. This is where students can finally focus on growth, mastery, and reaching their potential.

The Identification Process: What Need Are They Missing?

During my Master's program, one of my favorite courses was about psychology. After I understood Maslow's hierarchy, I started looking at student behavior differently. Instead of thinking, "Why is this student acting out?" I started asking, "What need isn't being met?"

Here's how to identify where a student might be stuck:

Signs a student is stuck at Physiological needs:

- Falling asleep in class
- Inability to focus
- Irritability or mood swings
- Frequently asking for food/snacks

Signs a student is stuck at Safety needs:

- Hypervigilance or anxiety
- Difficulty trusting adults
- Constant "testing" of boundaries
- Overreaction to small changes

Signs a student is stuck at Love and Belonging:

- Withdrawal or isolation
- Attention-seeking behavior
- Difficulty working in groups
- Extreme sensitivity to peer rejection

Signs a student is stuck at Esteem needs:

- Avoidance of challenging work
- Excessive need for validation
- Defensiveness about mistakes
- Giving up easily

Once you identify the level, you can respond with strategies instead of consequences. I took this course about three years ago, and to this day, I make decisions based on the signs listed above.

Sometimes, after getting to know my students, I will allow a student to put their head down for a moment because I know they had to go to the corner store at 9 p.m., by themselves, on foot, scared, to bring items home to their parents. They are tired. I know they have had to stay up all night and tend to their younger siblings because mom works late, and the student lives with a grandparent who can't do everything.

Susan's Story: The Resolution

With a student I will call Susan (for privacy), once I understood she was struggling with Love and Belonging, I made small adjustments.

I greeted her by name every day. I found moments to affirm her—not just her work, but her. I made sure she knew I saw her, valued her, and that she belonged in our classroom. I had her say daily affirmations when she entered the classroom (just loud enough that only she and I could hear).

I also connected her with our school counselor for additional support, because some needs are bigger than what I can meet alone.

Did she become a straight-A student overnight? No. But she started showing up—emotionally and academically. She began engaging, trusting, and once she felt like she belonged, she could finally start learning.

That's the power of understanding where students are and meeting them there.

That's the power of understanding where students are and meeting them there.

Challenge for You:

Think of your most disruptive student—or the one who's sometimes so quiet you don't even realize they're in the room. Where do you think they might be stuck on Maslow's hierarchy? Write down one small thing you could do to help meet that need.

Chapter 3

Consumption

Picture yourself eating a delicious meal. Not mindlessly shoveling food while scrolling on your phone—actually looking at what's on your plate. Tasting it. Experiencing it.

Most of the time, we see the food on our plates, but we're not really thinking about it. We're rushing. We're distracted. We're eating mindlessly while thinking about the million other things we need to do. Or, we're standing at the kitchen counter eating cold leftover pizza while grading papers *guilty smile*.

But not this time. For this meal, I want you to slow down. Pay attention. What does it taste like? How does it make you feel as you're eating? Stay with me—I promise this is going somewhere.

"Our bodies respond to what we consume."

Now imagine this meal is actually good for you. It's balanced. It includes veggies and protein, and the kind of nourishment your body needs. After you finish eating, how do you feel?

Compare that to how we feel after eating greasy, fatty, heavily processed, or fried food. When we fuel our bodies with food that lacks nourishment, often it's junk. We feel sluggish, irritable, or drained—sometimes without even realizing it. We often don't understand why we feel this way, but it's simply because our bodies respond to what we consume. I know that when I eat junk, I feel like junk, whether I realize it or not.

What we consume mentally and emotionally matter just as much as what we eat. Just as the food we put into our bodies affects our focus and emotional regulation, so do the words we speak, the conversations we engage in, and the messages from social media, TV, and radio that we repeatedly take in. They all shape our thinking, our energy, and how we show up each day.

Our bodies respond to what we consume—all of it.

The focus here is consumption related to self-care. The truth that is not widely addressed is that what we consume does not just mean the food we eat. To practice self-care, you have to be aware and mindful of the things you are consuming. Most of us don't even realize how much negativity we are consuming daily that takes away from our self-care.

Self-care is not only bubble baths, cold drinks, or time at the salon. It is taking care of your mind, body, and mental health. I want to challenge you to identify one task you can commit to completing every morning that is positive or helpful in some way, whether for your mind, body, or mental well-being. That is self-care.

Some people like to start their day with meditation, journaling, working out, or doing something creative. I like to begin my day with devotion and exercise, when time allows. What matters most is doing something positive that makes you feel good, because it often sets the tone for the rest of your day. This is healthy consumption.

Think about your mornings. Are you giving them away to the world by waking up and immediately scrolling through social media, checking text messages, and responding to emails? Or are you taking control of your mornings and being intentional about how your day begins? Slow mornings often make for the best mornings. Establishing a positive routine sets your day up for success. Be intentional about what you consume in the morning.

One thing that is very common, not only among teachers but across many industries, is complaining. Complaining happens often and daily, sometimes as soon as people walk into the school building early in the morning.

Consumption.

Complaining, or listening to complaints, is negative when there is no solution attached. Both drain your mental energy.

Consumption.

Just as junk food affects your body in a negative way, constant complaining affects your brain.

Consumption.

Negativity is contagious. The brain unconsciously absorbs the emotional states of those around it. Whether you are complaining or listening to others complain, stress responses are activated in both the speaker and the listener. Like junk food, complaining can feel familiar and comforting in the moment. Over time, however, it damages your system.

So what can you do about it?

Stop, or reduce, complaining.

The Brain Science Behind Complaining

What's happening: Repetitive complaining—whether it's your own or someone else's—physically rewires your brain. Each time you complain or listen to complaints, you strengthen neural pathways associated with negative thinking, making it easier for your brain to default to negativity the next time.

The impact isn't limited to the person complaining: Your brain unconsciously mimics the emotional states of people around you through something called neuronal mirroring. This means that just listening to complaints triggers the same harmful brain changes in you.

This includes but is not limited to:

- Elevated stress hormones
- Weakened cognitive function
- Strengthened negative thought patterns

Bottom line: Negativity truly is contagious, and your brain absorbs it whether you realize it or not.

Stop listening to complaints.

I remember one morning driving into work and sending a message to my team members. I issued a Monday morning challenge: you are not allowed to listen to anything negative. If someone came to you to complain, the challenge required you to say, "I'm sorry, but I'm doing a challenge, and I cannot listen to anything negative today." The purpose was to control consumption!

I had to put it into practice. I had to tell a student, "I'm sorry, but you cannot talk about that to me now. I'm in the middle of a challenge and I can't listen to anything negative."

The purpose was twofold. On one hand, I was controlling my consumption of negativity. But on the other hand, a deeper purpose was to make a difference. Imagine if everyone stopped consuming negativity— in the long run. If everyone simply stopped listening to complaints (complaints without solutions attached), because you choose what you listen to and what you don't. Your consumption is a choice.

What would end up happening is the people complaining would not have anyone to complain to. No one would engage, and I can pretty much guarantee the complaining would die down. It's a ripple effect. The consumption of negativity would decrease tremendously.

Positive Consumption

On the flip side of negative consumption, there is positive consumption. The choice is often easier to choose the junk over what's good for you, but the ultimate choice is yours. I want to share a few of the positive things I consume to bring them to your awareness. You may be consuming something similar, and you may just need more. It's all about balance. These things help me or contribute good to my life in some way.

My best friend, Belen, and I are both busy teachers, so when we get the chance to talk, we make it count. Some of my favorite moments are staying after work, standing by our vehicles in the parking lot, and sharing testimonies about all the amazing things God has done and is doing in our lives.

That's positive consumption.

When I watch YouTube videos, I'm watching something inspirational or motivational—something I often feel led to share with my family and coworkers.

That's positive consumption.

When I listen to podcasts, read books, or scroll social media, I'm intentional about what I'm letting into my mind.

That's positive consumption.

Here's the truth: Consuming positivity, and high amounts of it, allows you to pour that back out onto the people surrounding you.

You can't pour from an empty cup. But you also can't pour from a cup filled with poison caused by too much junk.

What you consume matters. What you consume is what you believe. What you believe shapes how you show up—for your students, for your loved ones, and for yourself. You have the right to protect what enters your mind and heart.

Pause. Notice what you're taking in. Tend to the roots.

JOURNALING PROMPT:

What are you feeding yourself? Aside from the food you eat, what are you consuming on a daily basis? (Think deeply, then write.)

_____

_____

_____

Chapter 4

Boundaries Are Self-Care

Are you the type of teacher who stays late because "it's easier to finish now"? The type of teacher who works at home because "it's just part of the job," or ignores headaches, tight shoulders, exhaustion, and irritability, and tells themselves, "I'll rest later"?

This teacher is strong. Reliable. Cares deeply. And is slowly disappearing from their own self.

Pushing through and working like this is often praised in teaching. We call it dedication, passion, commitment. I call it a lack of boundaries. And this was me...until it wasn't.

The Moment I Could Not Ignore Anymore

Since the year I began my teaching journey, I would work at school and bring my work home with me. At first, it felt normal—working from home to grade students' work, create worksheets, and design engaging lessons. However, the work itself was not the issue. The issue was that I was taking it home in addition to the extra hours I was putting in at school.

In my first year, I was the first one on campus and the last one to leave—right before (or with) the custodians.

Second-year me? New district, new school, yet still staying late and still working from home.

Third-year me? Same.

Fourth-year me was different. This was the year something changed.

My kids were getting older, elementary-aged. Yet, while at home, they did not just play alongside each other anymore—they wanted me. They wanted Mommy. To play. To sit. To be present.

I remember sitting at the kitchen table, laptop open, working on something I can't even remember now (and that should tell you how important it was). One of my kids asked me to play, and I said, "I can't. I have to work."

I teared up immediately. I closed my laptop and thought, never again.

It was at that moment I realized something, and everything changed. I didn't have to work at home. I was choosing to work at home. I was lacking boundaries. Realizing that it was a choice for me—that I was choosing to work from home—proved that I wasn't considering my self-care. I was normalizing overextension and blurring the lines between family and work. Boundaries needed to be set, and I was determined to set them.

The Brain Science Behind Boundaries

The inability to shift gears: Your nervous system has two main modes: sympathetic (fight-or-flight) and parasympathetic (rest-and-digest). Teaching keeps you in sympathetic mode, alert, reactive, managing behaviors, and making split-second decisions. Research on nervous system regulation shows that without clear boundaries between work and rest, your system can get stuck in fight-or-flight mode.

When this happens, you can't truly relax because your brain hasn't received the signal that the workday is over. This is why you may feel wired and exhausted at the same time.

Why boundaries improve your teaching: Studies on work-life balance and teacher effectiveness consistently show that teachers who set clear boundaries report higher job satisfaction, lower burnout rates, and—here's the key—better relationships with students. When you protect your recovery time, your prefrontal cortex can rest. You return to your classroom with better emotional regulation, clearer thinking, and more patience.

Bottom line: Neuroscience is clear—boundaries aren't optional if you want to sustain your career. Your brain needs recovery time to function at its best. Working through exhaustion doesn't make you a better teacher. It makes you a burned-out one.

What Boundaries Actually Look Like

After that moment with my kids, I made some clear decisions. I stopped grading at home. Period. I stopped looking at school emails on the weekend or after working hours. Period. I aimed to leave on time, but I gave myself grace if I needed to stay a little later one or two days a week.

And you know what? I felt no guilt. I began to feel lighter. The weight I had been carrying—the constant mental load of unfinished work, the nagging feeling that I should always be doing more—started to lift. I had space to breathe. I had time to be present with my kids. I had energy left for myself.

Boundaries are neurological protection. Boundaries are a form of self-respect and self-care for your nervous system. When you set boundaries, you protect your prefrontal cortex—the decision-making, emotional regulation area. You reduce your cortisol levels. You model what a healthy adult looks like for your students and for your own kids, if that applies to you. Ultimately, you make your career sustainable by avoiding burnout.

Set the boundaries.

Advice for Teachers Who Want to Set Boundaries (But Don't Know Where to Start)

If you're a new teacher—or even a seasoned one who's never set boundaries before—I want you to hear this: Stop worrying. Worrying causes stress. Save the work for your conference period, and whatever can't be done during that time can wait. Accept the fact that not everything will be finished, nor will it be perfect—and that's okay. Recognize what's happening, tend to the roots, and adjust as needed.

Start small. Pick one boundary and commit to it. Maybe it's no grading after dinner. Maybe it's no school emails on Sundays. Maybe it's leaving by 5 p.m. three days a week. Whatever it is, name it. Stick to it. Notice how it feels.

You might break a boundary sometimes. I have. I've stayed after school hours when I didn't plan to. But here's the difference: I didn't feel bad about it because I knew I was making the choice to stay, as opposed to feeling like I had to stay. That shift in mindset changes everything.

What About "Urgent" Situations?

You might be thinking, "But what about parent emails? What about last-minute admin requests? What if something urgent comes up?"

Here's what I've learned: urgent situations like parent emails and last-minute admin requests are not actually urgent. They should still be handled during school hours. After hours is my time. My family time. If I decide to handle a situation outside of hours, it's my choice, and the negative feelings typically aren't attached for that reason.

You get to decide what's truly urgent—that's boundaries. And most of the time, it can wait until tomorrow.

To the Teacher Who Believes "Good Teachers Sacrifice Everything"

If you believe that being a good teacher means sacrificing everything, I want you to stop and think about this: If you sacrifice everything, then you have nothing left in you to teach. *So how could you be good at anything if you've sacrificed everything?*

Let that sit with you for a moment...

You must fill your tank—emotionally, physically, and mentally—in order to be good for anyone else. That's self-care. If you have nothing left to give, you cannot be a "good teacher."

Put your mask on first so that you are able to help others. Recognize what's happening. Tend to the roots. Adjust as needed.

What Changed When I Set Boundaries

Burnout doesn't happen because teachers don't care, or because you have 2,000 unopened emails. Burnout happens because teachers care—and never learned where to stop.

My mom used to tell me, "The work will be there when you get back."

At that moment, I didn't believe it. I couldn't. I was in it. However, my work got done regardless of whether I did it at school or at home. I am here to tell you that my mom was right! My students didn't suffer when I stopped taking my work home. When I set boundaries, my children gained a present mom. And, most importantly, I gained myself back.

And you can too.

JOURNALING PROMPT:

What's one thing you've been telling yourself you "have to" do that is actually a choice? Write it down—then commit to protecting your time, your energy, and your peace.

_____

_____

_____

_____

_____

You are allowed to *stop pushing through*. You are allowed to choose yourself, because the work will still be there—but you won't be if you don't set boundaries.

In Chapters 1 and 2, we built the foundation. In Chapter 3, we protected what goes in. Now, in this chapter, we've learned to protect what goes out—our time, our energy, our presence. You cannot pour from an empty nervous system, and you don't get extra credit for running yourself into the ground.

Awareness comes first. Roots require care. Growth follows. Set the boundaries. Show up whole. That's how you perform at 100%—for you and for your students.

Chapter 5

The first weeks of school (Putting It All Together)

In Chapters 1-4, we discussed the roots, the true foundation: procedures, relationships, consumption, and boundaries. Now it's time to put it all into practice. Teaching doesn't happen in theory; it happens in the decisions you make in August, the resets you lead in November, and the stamina you build in April. In this chapter, I'm going to walk you through the most pivotal points in the school year, so you know exactly what to do and when.

Take yourself back to when you were hired—whether that was at the beginning or middle of the year. If you're brand new, about to begin your first year of teaching, consider this moment. The excitement, the fast heartbeat, and heavy breathing. The sweaty palms and pure nervousness, joy, and anxious feelings the first week before school starts. I can feel those emotions now as I'm writing this book. I can feel the jitters, the "what if" thoughts, and wondering what type of students I'll be blessed with in my classroom. Will I have students with learning disabilities, ADHD, students who aren't well-mannered or respectful? Will all my students be ready to learn and on the level I believe they should be? I wonder. Am I getting some sleepyheads? UGHHH!!! That feeling of not knowing, I can re-feel it now. To be honest, I have these same feelings before the beginning of every school year. *Transparency*

I am here to say, don't worry, because most likely you will have all the student types you're worrying about, because—that's life. Even if you don't have the variety of students in your classroom, you need to plan as though you will. We have no real control over who is on our roster or in our classroom. What is in our control is the environment we design before we receive our students. What we can control is our presentation of our classroom procedures and expectations. These you should have ready to go.

Before School Starts (What to Prepare)

- Get your treatment agreement template ready. This is just the framework we discussed in chapter 2, with the four questions:
    1. How should the students treat the teacher?
    2. How should the teacher treat the students?
    3. How should the students treat each other?
    4. How should we treat the classroom?

Your students will fill it in on day 1, you're just preparing the structure before.

- Create your slides that will explain your procedures
- Set up your space with some sort of visuals for your procedures
- Print out your procedures or have visual displayed so students can see

*Bonus: Another thing I would do before school starts is create office referral templates in a Google document. Depending on how your school handles referrals (ours are electronic), this may or may not work for you. But if it does, it's a game changer. It's really frustrating to have to type an office referral from scratch in the middle of class when that time could be better spent on something more impactful for your students. With templates already written for common reasons, all you need to do is add a name and adjust the details slightly.

Plan to introduce procedures using visuals like Canva or Google Slides. Students need to see and hear the procedures. Have them repeat these procedures to you, a partner, or within a group. Then, if possible, practice—this is how it sticks.

The Brain Science Behind Multi-Sensory Learning

Why visual + verbal + practice works: Educational neuroscience research shows that the brain learns best through multi-sensory input. When students see a procedure (visual), hear it explained (auditory), say it out loud (verbal production), and practice it (kinesthetic), they're encoding the information through multiple neural pathways. This creates stronger, more durable memories than passive listening alone.

The power of repetition and peer teaching: Studies on learning retention confirm that students remember:

- 10% of what they read

- 20% of what they hear

- 30% of what they see

- 50% of what they see and hear

- 70% of what they discuss with others

- 90% of what they teach to someone else

When students explain procedures to a partner or group, they're essentially teaching it— which research shows is the most effective way to learn and retain information.

Social learning and accountability: Research in educational psychology shows that peer interaction activates different parts of the brain than teacher-led instruction. When students discuss procedures with classmates, they're more likely to:

- Ask clarifying questions they might be too afraid to ask the teacher
- Process the information in their own words
- Feel accountable to their peers (social motivation)
- Retain the information longer

Bottom line: Research across learning science confirms that the "see it, say it, practice it" approach creates the strongest neural pathways and the highest retention rates. Multi-sensory learning isn't just good teaching— it's brain-based teaching.

Day 1 (The Foundation)

Let this be the day you create your treatment agreement with your students. The treatment agreement is vital—it forms the roots of your classroom culture. This agreement outlines how students will treat each other while in your classroom and how you will treat your students. It's easy for us as teachers to fuss at students for breaking an expectation, yet it's humbling to hold ourselves accountable to the expectations for how we should treat students.

Here's how it works:

You will already have the treatment agreement layout ready to present to the students. Have them work in groups or pairs to answer the four questions on a sheet of paper. At the end of the day, compile all feedback from the students and type it into the layout on your slide presentation. Yes, you will be tired, and yes, you will be ready to go home, but the payoff is immense.

Day 2

Pull up the treatment agreement slide and review everything in every category with your students as a class. Explain that this agreement is the foundation and sets the tone for how everyone will be treated from this point on. It's early in the year, so it's unlikely you will face any pushback from the students.

As you go over each section, ensure that all parties involved understand what each item means. You'd be surprised by what students come up with. In addition to validating their input, verify that you fully understand their meaning. For example, I had a student mention "personal space." I had to ask what exactly they meant. I allowed the student to explain, and I welcomed other input. The point is to ensure everyone has a shared understanding.

When you agree to a section, say "I agree." Go through each section and its affected parties. Ask if anyone has any questions, and be prepared to address them as they arise. Then, ask the class if they agree to treat each other this way (as you point to the sections that start with "the student"). It is imperative that you get a verbal "yes" from every single student because, from this point on, they will be held accountable. This is much different from my first year when I had everyone sign a bogus contract. *Laughing now.*

Week 1 (Practice, enforce)

What Week One does is set the bar for the remainder of the school year. This first week is essential for letting students know what you, as the teacher, will tolerate and what you will not. If your treatment agreement says "treat with respect," but you have a student being obviously disrespectful to their peers, they are watching to see whether you will redirect them. Their peers are watching as well.

If your agreement says "don't interrupt," then hold students accountable when they do. Refer to your treatment agreement. I have mine printed out on poster board and posted at the front of the room. There are no excuses.

If you tell your students to come in quietly, but they enter talking, and you don't address it or make any corrections, they will continue to disregard your expectations. However, if you redirect them every time they enter the classroom in a way that does not meet your expectations, they will eventually rise to the occasion.

Establish your roots and stay firm.

The first week of school enforces the expectations you've set.

Beyond presenting procedures and expectations

Depending on how you like your classes to flow, or if you're new to teaching, going over procedures gives your students a glimpse of what life in your class will be like this school year.

If you're a teacher who loves group work, this is a great time to have students discuss the expectations and procedures you've covered in small groups. If you prefer independent work, students can discuss the procedures on their own, if you choose. For those who enjoy partner work, have students discuss the procedures with a partner. Make it a thing. The purpose is for them to see it, say it, and practice it.

Practice. Practice. Practice

This is what I missed during my first two years! Have students physically stand up, exit the classroom, and re-enter as instructed. Have them talk about their summer break (and when you repeat the expectations after Thanksgiving or winter break, the conversation can focus on the recent break). Practice your procedure for gaining attention or using call-backs. We use a classroom bell.

The goal is to do the heavy lifting—explaining, practicing, and assessing understanding—at the beginning. This way, the procedures will either become second nature, or students can self-correct, freeing you from answering procedural questions.

Week 2 (reinforce expectations, and establish family connection)

In Week 2, continue reinforcing expectations. Continue modeling, practicing procedures, and getting families involved by contacting parents or guardians.

When contacting home about students who are not following expectations, this will serve two purposes:

1. It will give you insight into the family support available for that student.
2. It will show students that you are serious about your expectations.

The student will know that you and their family are on the same team. The good news is, most students who misbehave in the first week and have contact made with home will self-correct their behavior. This will make managing their behavior much easier for the rest of the school year.

It will also make future contact with this parent easier and less awkward because you've already made an initial connection within the first couple of weeks.

Weeks 3 Through Thanksgiving Break (stay consistent)

For the following weeks until Thanksgiving, continue to enforce expectations. You cannot back down! Stay consistent every day and continue practicing procedures. It must become a part of you and your students. Your expectations are not just words on a sheet of paper.

In Chapter 1, while trying to establish your expectations or procedures, your journaling prompt asked what is important to you. Please note that if it's not important to you, you will not stick with it, and it will not work.

After Thanksgiving Break (refresher)

When you return from Thanksgiving break, treat it like the first day of school. Re-explain, re-practice, and re-question your students to ensure they are still aware of your procedures and expectations. After more than a week off, students need that reset. The benefits of solid classroom management far outweigh the time it takes for this process.

After All Proceeding Breaks (reset and reassess)

I usually do this after every major break. What started as re-explaining, re-practicing, and re-questioning has now turned into a simple Google Form. In this form, I ask a question about every procedure and expectation that's important to me and our classroom culture.

I'm always amazed to see that even my typical troublemakers truly understand the expectations and procedures, according to their Google Form responses. So instead of taking time to practice, I'm simply taking an assessment to ensure they know the expectations and procedures.

In the worst case, I'm mentally prepared to practice expectations if most of the class fails the Google Form quiz *smiling while typing this*. But no class has failed yet. By this time in the school year, they do understand what you expect. Whether they abide by them or not is a different story *smiling*.

The Google Form submission can also serve as documentation for an office referral or parent communication, if needed. It provides evidence that the student truly understands what they are supposed to do but is choosing not to do the right thing.

JOURNALING PROMPT:

What Will Make You Want to Give Up on Consistency?
Be honest. Will it be:

- Exhaustion?

- Student pushback?

- Feeling like it's not working fast enough?

- Pressure from admin to move faster through content?

- Forgetting to enforce because you're overwhelmed?

Write down what you think your biggest obstacle will be. Then write one strategy for how you'll handle it when it shows up.

_____

_____

_____

_____

_____

Setting the Tone & Closing:

Establishing procedures and expectations is one thing. Following through is what makes them work. Consistency is what creates a sustainable classroom environment—not perfection, but showing up to the work over and over again.

Remember, students need to see it, say it, and practice it. That's how their brains learn. Reference your treatment agreement throughout the year, not just in August. Every time you reset, when you get a new student, and as situations arise when a reference is needed. It's the foundation of your classroom culture and the anchor for every relationship you build.

Set boundaries on what you consume and what your students consume. Align conversations with your treatment agreement. Strengthen relationships through consistency, not control.

You've built the foundation. Now trust it. You got this.

Chapter 6

When expectations and procedures fail

...because they will.

You have your perfectly set-out treatment agreement posted on the wall so that all students and yourself can see it at all times. You are in the middle of presenting an amazing lesson that you put together yesterday during your conference period (because we're not working from home), and a student decides to shout out "6-7!" and everyone begins to laugh.

Whoa!!!

Your thoughts immediately race: *Didn't I set the expectation that we are to be respectful while the teacher is talking? Didn't they agree to this?!* You are so frustrated, and it's at this exact moment that you have to make a decision that will impact far more than you can imagine.

Option 1: The Typical Road

This is the moment when you immediately recognize the laughing from the other students. Following that realization, you quickly turn and address the student who made the loud outburst. (In 2025, the phrase the kids said was "6-7." When you're reading this, it could be something else the kids are saying that you may not find too funny.) The point is, there was a distraction that took away from the lesson, and you are very upset. Which, under the circumstances, why wouldn't you be? You've been focused on your expectations and have praised the students for following through daily. I hope so, as this is also important, and you didn't go home to work on your lesson. Instead, you worked yesterday during your conference period. Now, a child is interrupting with some nonsense. Yes, you have the right to be upset.

In this option, you go off on that student. You tell the student, "EXCUSE ME! DIDN'T YOUR MOMMA RAISE YOU RIGHT TO KNOW YOU ARE NOT SUPPOSED TO INTERRUPT WHEN I AM TALKING! YOU ALWAYS DO THIS AND IT'S NOT ACCEPTABLE! I'M SO TIRED OF YOUR DISRESPECT AND LACK OF CARE. THIS IS WHY YOUR GRADES ARE SO LOW!"

And while you yell, the others are still laughing. But now, they are not laughing with the student who made the outburst. They are now laughing at you for losing your cool.

The Brain Science Behind Option 1:

What's happening in the student's brain: When you call them out publicly, their amygdala (the threat detection center) activates immediately. The brain perceives public humiliation as a survival threat. The prefrontal cortex — responsible for reflection, remorse, and learning — shuts down completely. The student can't process your message because their brain has shifted into fight-or-flight mode. Research on adolescent brain development shows that public shaming reinforces defensive behavior patterns rather than correcting them.

What's happening in the other students' brains: Mirror neurons cause the entire class to experience your emotional dysregulation. When you lose control, their nervous systems detect, "The adult isn't safe right now." Studies on classroom climate show that when teachers publicly shame students, the whole class's stress hormones (cortisol) spike. Learning stops. The brain can't learn when it feels unsafe.

What's happening in your brain (the teacher): Your amygdala has hijacked your prefrontal cortex. You're operating from your reactive brain, not your thinking brain. Neuroscience shows that when we're dysregulated, we model dysregulation — teaching students that when you're upset, you explode. This erodes the treatment agreement you built together.

Bottom line: Public confrontation activates everyone's threat response and shuts down learning. Private redirection keeps everyone's prefrontal cortex online — the student can reflect, the class can learn, and you stay regulated. Dignity protects the relationship. And the relationship is what makes everything else work.

I remember a few years ago sitting in a professional development session with Brian Mendler, the author of the book That One Kid, and my perspective was changed as I listened to him. Brian was that one kid — the one looking for attention, showing off in front of his friends. It was during that session that I realized, oh my goodness, this is a show! For the students.

OOHHHH, this is what they (whoever "they" are) meant when they said "praise in public, discipline in private."

Ever since I came to this realization, my classroom has changed, for the better.

Option 2: A Different Path

Look at that student. Quietly and quickly, ask that student to step outside and continue teaching for a moment. Just a moment. The best option would be to continue teaching over the laughter for a few seconds, just while you're walking to the disruptive student. And just to them — no one else can hear you — TELL that student to step outside.

Yes, they will probably mumble something to make you upset (Brian's examples are hilarious, you have to check him out), and they may make a face. But you have to know this: they are kids.

You will be so surprised to know that as soon as that student is halfway out and you have continued teaching (for just a moment), how quiet your room will get.

You must try it and experience it for yourself.

The Brain Science Behind Option 2:

What's happening in the student's brain: A quiet, private conversation keeps their prefrontal cortex online. Research shows that when correction happens privately, students are more likely to reflect on their behavior rather than defend their ego. Their brain isn't flooded with shame and cortisol. They can actually hear you and process what you're saying. Developmental psychology confirms that students respond better to private correction because it protects their social status with peers.

What's happening in the other students' brains: When you calmly redirect and keep teaching, you send a powerful message: "I'm in control. We're okay." Their nervous systems stay regulated. Studies on classroom management show that students feel safer when teachers handle disruptions calmly and privately. The class sees: "This teacher doesn't embarrass people. This teacher handles things with dignity." The show is over — and there's nothing to laugh at.

What's happening in your brain (the teacher): Taking a breath and choosing the private conversation activates your prefrontal cortex. You're responding, not reacting. Neuroscience shows that pausing — even for just a few seconds — allows your thinking brain to come back online. You're modeling emotional regulation. Research on teacher wellbeing confirms that teachers who use calm, private redirection experience less burnout and report higher job satisfaction — because they're not carrying the emotional weight of explosive confrontations.

Bottom line: Public confrontation activates everyone's threat response and shuts down learning. Private redirection keeps everyone's prefrontal cortex online — the student can reflect, the class can learn, and you stay regulated. Dignity protects the relationship, and the relationship is what makes everything else work.

The thing is, it takes humbling yourself. Yes, you are the adult, and yes, you are technically in charge, but remember the relationship building and the foundation. It does not work unless it goes both ways. You have to uphold your end of the bargain as well, and I would not be surprised to see what some of your students come up with regarding how they want their teacher to treat them.

Think about the route you would typically take. What reactions are you faced with? Does your blood pressure rise when you're upset? Imagine pulling that student outside and modeling three deep breaths so that both of you can calm down. I can tell you from experience, it's amazing! Not only does this allow me to calm down before I go off on this student, but it also allows them to calm down so they can be open to accepting whatever I have to say.

Since I am calm, I am not out there fussing at them. However, I am reminding them about the treatment agreement we all agreed to, and I am explaining to this student/child whatever my feelings may be. If they are accepting of that, great. If not, I will just let them know how their actions are taking away from the learning of others and how what they are doing is not fair to me. Nine out of ten times, it will work. The student is not surrounded by an audience, so they are no longer performing — as long as you're not putting on a show. They are following your lead.

I say nine out of ten because I do this with my students at least once per class period for the first couple of weeks. Then it always dies down to about once or twice a day. Now that I am writing this book mid-school year, it's maybe a few times a month that I have to pull a student outside. Because the trust is gained. They know I am not trying to embarrass them in front of their friends. They know I am not going to allow them to put on a SHOW because the moment there seems to ALMOST be an issue, I'm going to politely tell them to step outside and I'm going to continue my teaching (for a moment) before I step into the hallway to address them.

It's only been maybe… I'm trying to think, but I'm having a hard time… one student that was not receptive. But honestly, I can't think of a time when I did this and it didn't go in my favor. It's amazing how, when we cherish the dignity of our students, they will perform for us in our classroom and presence.

JOURNALING PROMPT:

What would stop you from disciplining privately (just you and the student, in front of cameras, of course) instead of in the classroom, loudly, and putting on a show (because that's what it is)? Take your time and answer honestly.

_____

_____

_____

_____

_____

Choosing Option 2 Beyond the Classroom

Here's the thing: choosing option 2 isn't just about classroom management. It's a mindset that changes how you move through the world. This whole "choosing" thing goes beyond the classroom.

I was sitting in Starbucks writing this book, actually, when I simply asked if my drink was ready.

If you can imagine me sitting at a table facing the baristas, laptop open, fully engrossed in what I am putting on these pages. Headphones in because calm music with no words helps me focus (find your thing that helps you), so I can't hear anyone if they did try to call me. But they wouldn't, because the lady who took my order never asked me for my name. So, since I know from experience, they let my items sit on the counter and never tell me personally (I'm here writing often — smile), I got up to ask if my drink was ready. I proceeded to add, "You never asked me for my name."

In all my years of coming to this particular Starbucks — mind you, it's been over 18 years — I have never had anyone who was rude.

Another lady heard me, looked over, and very dramatically rolled her eyes and said, "WHAT?" I wish I could add a visual description here for you to see how much of an eye roll and attitude was given to me.

I think on a typical day, I would have maybe — just maybe — said something to the supervisor or something. However, today I chose option 2. I literally sat down, went back to writing, and told myself, "Choose option 2."

Now, I didn't ask her to step outside so we could address this situation ::laughing now::, but I did take it upon myself to realize that I could not control that young lady and her emotions since she was not a student or a child of mine. However, I could control my own emotions and how I handled that situation.

Think beyond the classroom with this. What is going to be affected and what is truly going to matter in the long run? This is her job, and when I leave, she will still be here working, minding her own business, and doing what she will continue to do. Getting attitudes with others most likely will be in the mix, but that is out of my control.

I had an expectation, and it was not met in this situation. I chose option 2 and controlled my emotions. To be honest, I had to take some deep breaths and tell myself not to allow her to make me upset.

We have to do this several times throughout the day. Recognize what triggers you. Recognize your feelings and emotions. We are human, and we will have valid emotions. It's what you do with them that makes a difference.

Troubleshooting Procedures

When students don't follow procedures — the way things are done — just remind them or point them to where you have your procedures printed on the wall so they can read for themselves. Don't make procedures a fight. We must remember that the prefrontal cortex isn't developed until their 20s. Have a little grace. Teach, model, and practice procedures.

This is a super humbling chapter, but the amazing feeling you will receive if you begin to make some minor adjustments in your delivery is worth it. Practice, because trust me, it doesn't come easy right away. Practice modeling self-control.

For me, it started with the treatment agreement. One year (my third year of teaching), one of my students answered the question, "How should the teacher treat the students?" with "Do not yell at us."

To be completely honest with you, that was a personal goal — and only personal. I hadn't even told my husband. I don't even think I spoke the words out loud. My goal was to try not to yell as much, you know, because I was going home with no voice from yelling the year before on a daily basis. I wanted to do better, personally.

(Laughing now.) To my surprise, it ended up on our treatment agreement, which then held me accountable to my personal goal. What a trip.

I was honest with my students as well, because honesty builds trust. I told them that this was going to be difficult for me, so I asked them for help. I said, "If you see me get upset, please tell me to take deep breaths." This was so I could calm down. Little did I know, I was modeling to them how to calm down.

From my first year of implementation, when the students would tell me, "Calm down, Mrs. Tupou," fast forward a few years, and now they don't have to tell me. Instead, I tell them, "Hold on, I'm calming down. Someone just made me very upset. Just give me a moment." They wait and watch (because what in the world, lol), and then I explain, "I was so upset with this person, so I have to calm down. We all get upset, right? Y'all get upset with your friends, and adults also get upset. We can take deep breaths to calm down." Or something to that nature in conversation.

Honestly, it's been an amazing transformation I've seen in myself and my classrooms over the years. So, the students not only take deep breaths with me in the hallway before we have tough conversations, but they also see me modeling calming down in the classroom when I'm upset. So, it's not too out of the ordinary.

Practice humbling yourself, and you will be amazed at the outcome. When you choose dignity over drama — both for your students and for yourself — you're not just managing behavior. You're building the kind of classroom where everyone's nervous system can stay calm enough to learn.

JOURNALING PROMPT:

Before your next challenging moment happens (and it will), write down your commitment: "When a student disrupts my lesson, I will

_____

_____

_____

_____

_____ "

Be specific. Will you pause and breathe? Step into the hallway? Keep teaching for a moment? Decide NOW, so you're not deciding in the heat of the moment. Plan to stick to it! Take a picture of this prompt, print it out, and keep it near your desk as a constant reminder.

Chapter 7

Sustain Yourself Daily

Self-care often feels like one more thing on the to-do list. But self-care AT WORK is different. It's micro-moments that sustain you. In this chapter, I am sharing strategies from my own PD sessions that teachers loved — practical tools you can use between classes, during planning, or when you're about to lose it.

The Power of Micro-Moments

You don't need hours at the spa or gym. You need two minutes and some space. For me, that space is the hallway. You need a few minutes and some coloring utensils. You need simple, accessible strategies that fit into your actual day. Nothing extra.

The Brain Science Behind Micro-Moments of Self-Care

Why micro-moments work: Research in stress psychology shows that brief moments of intentional self-care — even 2-5 minutes — can reset the nervous system and reduce cortisol levels. Studies on mindfulness and movement confirm that short breaks improve focus, emotional regulation, and decision-making.

Bottom line: Your brain doesn't need hours to recover; it needs consistent, intentional pauses throughout the day.

The Day I Discovered I'm Not Superhuman

Oh my GOODNESS! How true is this?

When I first experienced this micro-moment, I was so overwhelmed. If you were a fly on the wall in my classroom that particular day, you would probably have cried a little puddle on the floor from laughter. I was a mess! Walking in circles around my desk, board, and panel, with what seemed like a grocery list of to-dos and about 17 tabs open on my computer. No lie. And it... it was a mess.

Something internal told me to put my headphones on and go walk around the hallway for a moment. Honestly, it was less than five minutes.

When I got back to my classroom, it was amazing! I was so focused and able to complete one task at a time. I thought I hit the mother lode, gold! But it's pure science. Read the grey box above if you haven't already. But yesss. I was super excited to have the opportunity to share this gold with the teachers who worked with me. And I'm more excited to now share it with you.

The Self-Care PD

My best friend and I were offered the opportunity to co-lead a teacher staff development session of our choice. We chose self-care as the topic, along with demonstrating to teachers how we run stations in our classroom. The goal of this session was for teachers to leave with strategies that could be implemented right away for their classroom student transitions, as well as their self-care management at work. (Smiling now.) I'm excited to share this session with you.

The response was overwhelming. Teachers told us:

"This session was just what I needed." — T. Oliva

"This session was the best all day." — Mr. Briggs

"This session was a much-needed lesson for those who needed to find ways to implement self-care throughout their normal days/duties." — Mr. Bell

These weren't just nice words — teachers were experiencing something they'd been craving: practical self-care that fit into their actual workday.

***We had three stations in our session, so this chapter will be split in that structure.

Station 1: Draw Your Stress and Color It Away

This station was one of the most popular stations in our PD. Teachers were skeptical at first, not thinking they had time. But as soon as the timer started, the room was calm. Focused. Quiet.

"This station was relaxing. It provided ways to relieve stress and tension in a work environment." — S. York

"I particularly enjoyed the part where we had to draw out our feelings...It made me take a step back and realize how far I've come these past couple of years." — Ms. Martinez-Salinas

How It Works

Part 1: Draw Your Stress (2-3 minutes at most)

Take a few quiet moments to reflect on what stress feels like for you as an educator. Think about what causes it, how it shows up in your day, or how it feels in your body or mind. Now, without worrying about artistic skill, use shapes, colors, symbols, or scenes to draw your stress.

Part 2: Color the Stress Away (5-10 minutes at most)

Now take a moment to color the stress away. We provided coloring pages with intricate patterns — mandalas, geometric designs — as well as coloring pencils. Just color. No thinking. Just breathe and color.

Why This Works:

Coloring activates the prefrontal cortex while quieting the amygdala (your stress center). It's a form of active meditation — your hands are busy, so your mind can rest. Drawing your stress first allows you to name it, acknowledge it, and then symbolically release it through coloring.

How to Use It at Work:

- Keep coloring pages and pencils in your desk (a companion book with nothing but coloring pages will be released one day)
- Use during planning period, lunch, or before/after school — or even during two out of five of those minutes at the beginning of your class period, since you have created that time for you before your lesson
- Set a timer for 5 minutes — you don't need long

Station 2: Journaling Task Cards

The second station was journaling, but not the "dear diary" kind. These were focused prompts designed to help teachers process emotions, ground themselves, or release stress in just a few minutes.

Teachers responded powerfully to these prompts:

"The journaling prompts helped me process how I felt about my current blessings and struggles." — P. Jasso
"I really like the self-care task cards. I love the task cards." — S. Leger
"Station 2 was definitely a reflective piece as it was difficult to choose a task. Many of them really resonated with me, and I could have done a majority of them."

I have since been asked for the task cards that we used for this station by several teachers. One was a reading specialist who used them at another staff development and received amazing feedback from the teachers she worked with. I was also asked by a social studies and reading teacher for the cards to use with whomever they chose.

How It Works:

In this station, there are several journaling prompts organized by purpose. Find one that pulls on your heartstrings and begin to write. Go at your own pace, speed, and style. The task cards are prompts and meant to be used for self-reflection and practicing the art of journaling. You don't have to fill pages — sometimes one or two sentences is enough.

Prompts:

For Grounding and Gratitude:

What are three small things that brought you comfort or joy today?

_____

_____

_____

_____

_____

_____

What is something about your body or mind that you are grateful
for right now?

_____

_____

_____

_____

_____

Describe a recent moment when you felt completely present and
at peace.

_____

_____

_____

_____

_____

_____

_____

For Processing Emotions:

What would I say to a friend who was feeling the way I am feeling right now?

What's one thing I've been avoiding thinking about, and what makes it feel hard to face?

For Self-Compassion:

What's something difficult I'm going through, and how can I be kinder to myself about it?

_____

_____

_____

_____

_____

Write a letter to yourself from the perspective of someone who loves you unconditionally.

_____

_____

_____

_____

_____

For Reflection and Growth:

When did I feel most like myself recently, and what was I doing?

_____

_____

_____

_____

_____

_____

What does rest look like for me? Am I getting enough of it?

_____

_____

_____

_____

_____

For Releasing Stress:

What thoughts are taking up the most mental space right now? Just dump them all on the page.

_____

_____

_____

_____

_____

_____

What's one small thing I can control today, even when so much feels out of my control?

_____

_____

_____

_____

_____

_____

If this stressful situation were happening to someone else, what advice would I give them?

_____

_____

_____

_____

_____

_____

_____

_____

Stream of Consciousness:

Finish this sentence and keep writing: If I'm being completely honest with myself...

_____

_____

_____

_____

_____

_____

_____

Finish the sentence and keep writing: What I really want to say but I haven't said out loud is...

_____

_____

_____

_____

_____

_____

What are you still carrying that you're ready to put down? Explore what that weight feels like and what letting go might mean.

_____

_____

_____

_____

_____

_____

_____

What would you do differently if you trusted yourself completely?

_____

_____

_____

_____

_____

_____

How to Use It:

- Use it here, now — pick one prompt and write for a couple of minutes
- Dog-ear these pages and come to them when you need a moment
- Keep a separate journal and copy prompts that resonate
- Schedule time (5 minutes) during your planning period for reflection
- Use these prompts as morning pages before students arrive, or during the 5 minutes as soon as they leave for the day (if you don't have after-school duty)

Station 3: The Walk

This was the simplest station — and maybe the most powerful.

In this station, teachers were faced with a seemingly difficult task in front of them. They were told to just look at the task, without thinking, and give me their initial reactions. I wanted feelings. The responses I got were: "too many words," "I don't wanna do it," "too much work," "confusing," "complicated," "overwhelming," "stressed," "headache," and my favorite responses were "I'm done" and "NOPE"... lol, that's just to name a few.

The teachers were guided to leave the task on the desk and head to the hallway. I then suggested that anyone with a smartwatch go ahead and start a workout. The looks of confusion were awesome. Some things I overheard:

"Why are we starting a workout?"

"What are we doing? This is the middle of the day."

"I've never used the workout app on my watch before."

I loved the curiosity.

We began to walk. As we started, I told them that this was the station. There was relief and a little laughter, which is always good for the soul. I proceeded to tell the teachers and staff that this is what I do for self-care at work. As we walked the halls of our school, this was my conversation:

"There was one day when I was severely overwhelmed. There was beginning-of-the-year data due, grades, and several other items on my forever to-do list. I literally had over 10 tabs open on my computer, and for some reason, I could not focus on one thing at a time. I was overwhelmed. Something led me to step out into the hallway, pop in my headphones, and take a walk around the circle (the hallway in our school). After a few minutes, I came back to my room, and I was able to focus on my task with no issues. I literally felt so good. I have been doing this every time I feel overwhelmed. When I return to my classroom, I feel amazing. The task I gave you was a representation of the overwhelming things we have in front of us sometimes on a daily basis. But this walk is a reminder that we can show a little self-care even in our busiest times. My shortest walk was about two minutes, and the longest about 20, depending on my conference time. It's well worth the minutes walking to come back and be productive than to spend double the time being unproductive."

When we returned to the room and took a closer look at the task, the directions were much clearer. We were to complete a vision board with things the teachers personally enjoyed — colors, smells, pictures, and things that brought them joy. The point was to take what was on the vision board and add these elements to their space. Space is within our control, and our environment shapes how we feel on a daily basis, which is also part of self-care. Making sure you feel good in your space will, in turn, allow students to feel good in your space as well.

Teachers discovered the power of intentional movement that day. Here's some of the feedback:

"The going for a walk idea, I really appreciated because sometimes that's all you need to decompress." — Mr. Bell

"I enjoyed the walk that Mrs. Tupou made us go on around the school. She showed us what she does to release the stress of the day simply through a quick walk around the building." — Ms. Martinez-Salinas

"How important 5 minutes away from your desk is to your overall being."

If you have the time now, I recommend you dog-ear this page. Set a timer for 5 minutes and then return.

Stepping away from a task to walk is amazing. It resets me. All of the deadlines, meeting preparations, contacting parents, grading papers, and everything else we need to do at our desk can become overwhelming at times. It causes stress, and we simply need a break. Take the 2 minutes, the 5 minutes — whatever you can afford — and get back to your classroom. Then, do the task.

Here's How to Do It: The Walk

Before you walk, write down the things you need to do — maybe in order, maybe not. But write them down and leave them visible on your desk. In just a moment, you will go for a 2-minute walk, return to your desk, and complete one task on the list.

It will not work if you:

- Stop and talk to people in the hallway
- Think about all the things you need to get complete

It will work if you:

- Clear your mind on your walk

- Listen to a podcast or some uplifting music while you walk
- Read a book while you walk
- JUST WALK

When you return to your desk, complete one thing on the list.

The Brain Science Behind Walking

Why does it seem easier to complete the task after we walk?

Why movement resets your brain: Neuroscience research shows that movement — even brief walking — increases blood flow to the prefrontal cortex, improving focus and decision-making. Studies on exercise and cognition confirm that just 2-5 minutes of movement can reduce cortisol, increase endorphins, and reset emotional dysregulation.

The attention restoration effect: Research in environmental psychology shows that walking (especially if you can see nature or change your environment) gives your brain a break from directed attention. This allows your attentional resources to restore, making complex tasks feel easier when you return.

Why the task feels easier after walking: Your brain needs a reset. When you're overwhelmed, your prefrontal cortex gets overloaded. Walking gives it a micro-break, allowing it to reorganize and approach the task with fresh cognitive resources. It's not that the task got easier — your brain got clearer.

Bottom line: Walking isn't procrastination — it's cognitive preparation. Studies show that brief movement breaks improve productivity, creativity, and problem-solving.

Making It Sustainable

Here's what teachers said about the overall impact:

"I wish there was more time for each station!"

"The ability to sit, reflect, and express myself was a nice change up." — L. Martinez

"Eye-opening!" — P. Jasso

"This session taught me how to decompress."

"I learned the importance of taking a mental break and how it can positively impact your day." — Ms. Martinez-Salinas

"I learned how to release stress."

"This session created a sense of reflection and rethinking."

"This session was educational and relaxing."

I know what you're thinking: "I don't have time for this." But here's the truth. You don't have time NOT to do this. Two minutes of coloring saves you 20 minutes of recovering from a meltdown. Five minutes of journaling prevents an hour of ruminating at home. A 90-second walk refocuses you faster than scrolling your phone for 10 minutes.

Pick 1-2 strategies that resonate with you. Try them for a week and pay attention to what shifts. You don't have to do it all — just find what works for YOU.

JOURNALING PROMPT:

What's one self-care strategy from this chapter that you tried or are willing to try this week? Write it down. Commit to it. Your nervous system will thank you.

_____

_____

_____

_____

_____

In Chapters 1-4, we built the foundation with procedures, relationships, consumption, and boundaries. In Chapters 5-6, we put it into practice: how to teach and how to troubleshoot. Now, in this chapter, you've learned how to sustain yourself through the daily grind.

Self-care at work isn't selfish — it's survival. It's what allows you to show up whole, grounded, and ready for your students every single day.

You cannot pour from an empty nervous system. Protect moments of calm throughout your day—these micro moments are your roots that sustain you. When you protect your roots, you protect your foundation. Your students need you — but you need you first.

Chapter 8

The Foundation You've Built

This has been an amazing journey, speaking with you through the words on these pages.

If it seems like it's too much to do — what I'm talking about in this book — consider the cost. What are you costing yourself without a positive foundation?

You're costing yourself daily stress that could have been avoided. You are probably complaining every day, creating negative input that's affecting your output. You are also probably not being honest with yourself in some way or another.

But if you've made it this far, I can assume that deep in your heart, you want to be an amazing teacher. And you can be. You are!

You just need to know it. You need to speak it into yourself — how amazing you are. Go back and engage with the journaling prompts. Take a look into what bothers you in your classroom. Address the culture you've created in your room. Are you holding yourself to the same standards as you hold your students to? Do you get upset easily and expect your students to stay calm?

How about the teacher who comes in every morning, waving with a smile on their face, greeting students excitedly: "Good morning! Good morning! Good morning!" (Smile.) That's me most days. And that can definitely be you.

It's all about perspective.

I don't know about you, but I'm so grateful to have a job — especially knowing how many people want one but can't. I am grateful to have a career that I don't feel is work. It's fun. It's always engaging me and keeping me on my toes.

Always being willing to learn and adjust is what will keep you in a constant state of joy. Joy is something that does not come and go as easily as happiness. You can be happy for one moment, then something happens and you are no longer happy. But joy is a deeper thing. Joy goes beyond the surface. And it's that joy that allows me to walk into my job smiling because I'm genuinely blessed to be there.

The Brain Science of Joy vs. Happiness

There's a reason joy feels different than happiness — and it's not just poetic. Neuroscience shows us that happiness and joy activate different pathways in the brain.

Happiness is often tied to dopamine — the "reward" neurotransmitter. It spikes when something good happens (a compliment, a fun weekend, a student's breakthrough), but it fades quickly. Dopamine is powerful, but fleeting.

Joy, on the other hand, is linked to serotonin and oxytocin — neurotransmitters associated with contentment, connection, and emotional stability. Joy doesn't come from external rewards; it comes from meaning, purpose, and gratitude. And here's the key: joy is sustainable.

Research shows that teachers who regularly practice gratitude — even something as simple as naming three things they're grateful for each day — experience:

- Lower cortisol levels (less stress)
- Increased resilience during difficult moments
- Stronger relationships with students and colleagues

Gratitude literally rewires your brain through neuroplasticity. The more you practice noticing what's good, the more your brain learns to default to that perspective — even on hard days.

Bottom line: Perspective isn't just a nice idea. It's biology. And you can train your brain to choose joy.

It's all perspective. First day of school, first week of school, first few months of school — you could take the perspective that this is too much, and you could choose to complain. Or, you can take the perspective that you get to have a job to come to every day. You can choose to take the mini self-care steps throughout the workday to allow yourself to function.

You can set yourself up with your procedures and expectations so that you get the first five minutes of every class. You can choose what inputs you have, what you consume on a daily basis — that's your choice. When your students choose to disrupt your lesson, choose option two. Choose the option where you're the model of self-regulation. Because not only are you showing your students how to maintain their self-control, but you also allow yourself to calm down. And over time, this leads to sustainability.

Did you read the grey boxes and understand how students' brains, as well as yours, work? I believe that if you put in the effort in the beginning — the foundation — and build from there, your output will be absolutely amazing.

Imagine students no longer wanting to stay home from school or skip your class because of their feelings. Imagine having such an amazing, welcoming, comforting environment that nurtures students to learn, and they want to be there every day. Imagine every classroom and every teacher being this way. Students want to come to school. If we each change and adapt to the needs of the students we serve... imagine the shift in education.

One day, these kids will be taking care of us.

The Roots That Hold You

Everything we've covered in this book—the procedures, the relationships, the boundaries, the self-care—these aren't just strategies. They're your roots. Just like a tree needs strong roots to weather the storms and grow tall, you need these foundations to sustain your teaching career. When your roots are strong, you can bend without breaking. You can thrive, not just survive.

The procedures give you mental clarity—roots that create space for learning.

The relationships build trust—roots that anchor your classroom culture.
The boundaries protect your energy—roots that keep you grounded.

The self-care sustains you daily—roots that nourish you from within.

When you protect these roots, you protect everything that grows from them: your joy, your impact, your longevity in this profession. This is what it means to be rooted.

Tomorrow Morning...

Whether you're reading this in July with a fresh school year ahead, in December needing a reset, or in May wondering if you can make it one more year — the foundation still matters. You can start, or restart, anytime.

You don't have to do all of this at once. Pick one thing. Start small. Whether that's tomorrow, next week, or when school starts in the fall — just start.

If you're reading this in the summer, use this time to build your foundation before the chaos starts. If you're reading mid-year or at the end of a long semester, know this: it's never too late to shift. You can reset your classroom culture. You can reclaim your joy. You can start fresh — even in March.

The foundation you've built through these chapters — the procedures, the relationships, the boundaries, the self-care — isn't just about surviving the school year. It's about creating a classroom where both you and your students can thrive.

You've learned how to protect your energy, build trust, manage stress, and show up whole. You've learned that teaching doesn't have to drain you. It can sustain you — if you're rooted in the right foundation.

So here's my challenge to you: Choose one thing from this book. One procedure. One boundary. One self-care practice. One moment of choosing option two. Start there. Build from there. Because you deserve to love teaching again. Your students deserve a teacher who shows up grounded, calm, and present. And education deserves teachers like you — teachers who are willing to do the work, build the foundation, and stay rooted. Thank you for trusting me with your time and your heart through these pages. I'm rooting for you.

Now go build something beautiful.

References & Further reading

This book draws on research from educational psychology, neuroscience, and classroom management studies. Below are key sources that informed the brain science sections and strategies throughout.

These resources provide evidence-based insights that can transform your practice.

Chapter 1: Procedures

- Wong, H. K., & Wong, R. T. (2018). *The First Days of School: How to Be an Effective Teacher* (5th ed.). Harry K. Wong Publications.

Chapter 2: Relationships

- Maslow, A. H. (1943). "A Theory of Human Motivation." *Psychological Review*, 50(4), 370-396.
- Perry, B. D., & Szalavitz, M. (2017). *The Boy Who Was Raised as a Dog: And Other Tales from a Child Psychiatrist's Notebook*. Basic Books.

Chapter 3: Consumption

- Hanson, R. (2013). *Hardwiring Happiness: The New Brain Science of Contentment, Calm, and Confidence*. Harmony Books

Chapter 4: Boundaries

- Porges, S. W. (2011). *The Polyvagal Theory*. Norton.

Chapter 5: First Weeks of School

- Steinberg, L. (2014). *Age of Opportunity: Lessons from the New Science of Adolescence*. Houghton Mifflin Harcourt.
- Wong, H. K., & Wong, R. T. (2018). *The First Days of School: How to Be an Effective Teacher* (5th ed.). Harry K. Wong Publications.

Chapter 6: When Things Fall Apart

- Siegel, D. J., & Bryson, T. P. (2011). *The Whole-Brain Child: 12 Revolutionary Strategies to Nurture Your Child's Developing Mind*. Bantam.
- LeDoux, J. E. (2015). *Anxious: Using the Brain to Understand and Treat Fear and Anxiety*. Viking.

Chapter 7: Sustaining Yourself Daily

- Hanson, R. (2013). *Hardwiring Happiness: The New Brain Science of Contentment, Calm, and Confidence*. Harmony Books.

Chapter 8: The Foundation You've Built

- Fredrickson, B. L. (2009). *Positivity: Top-Notch Research Reveals the Upward Spiral That Will Change Your Life*. Harmony Books.

Your voice matters

This book was written to be **used**—dog-eared, highlighted, written in, and returned to again and again. If it has helped you in any way, I'd love to hear about it.

What resonated with you most?

Whether you're a first-year teacher finding your footing, a veteran educator looking for renewal, or anywhere in between —your experience matters.

Please scan the QR code below to share your thoughts:

https://bit.ly/rootedinput

Thank you for trusting me with your time and your heart. I'm rooting for you

— Sharde' Tupou